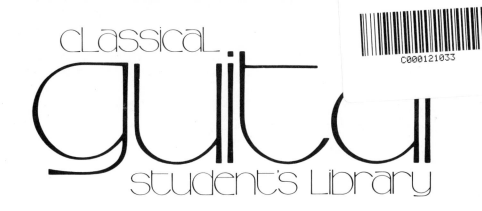

classical guitar student's library

popular collection

CONTENTS

215-2-346

Selected, Edited & Arranged by Ivor Mairants

First Published 1986
© International Music Publications

Exclusive Distributors
International Music Publications
Southend Road, Woodford Green,
Essex IG8 8HN, England.

Printed in England by Loader Jackson Printers Ltd.,
Arlesey, Bedfordshire

LEFT HAND MARKINGS

1) Numbers beside, above or below the notes denote the fingers to be used.
1 = index finger 2 = middle finger 3 = ring finger 4 = little finger. When the same finger number applies to more than one note that finger must be placed across the frets. This is known as a barré, i.e. barring the strings.

2) A number inside a ring indicates that notes so marked must be played on the required string ② = second string ④ = fourth string etc.

3) A Roman numeral above a note or phrase indicates the fingerboard position of those notes or chords and when the Roman numeral has the letter C in front of it, e.g. **CIV**, it means the first finger must barré across the fourth fret, with the other fingers in their relative positions.

4) The diagrams represent the fingerboard, the longitudinal lines the strings and the lateral lines the frets.

Unless there is a number on the left hand side of the box opposite a lateral line which denotes the fret number, the top line represents the nut, the next line = 1st fret and so on.

When there *is* a number beside a line *that* is the fret at which the first finger is placed.

The figures *above* the diagram represent the fingerings on each of the strings.

1, 2, 3 and 4 = the first, second, third and fourth fingers o = an open string. X means do not sound that string. In addition to the diagrams there are, of course, the chord symbols.

Autumn Leaves
(Les Feuilles Mortes)

Original Lyrics by Jacques Prevert
English Lyrics by Johnny Mercer
Additional verse by Geoffrey Parsons
Music by Joseph Kosma

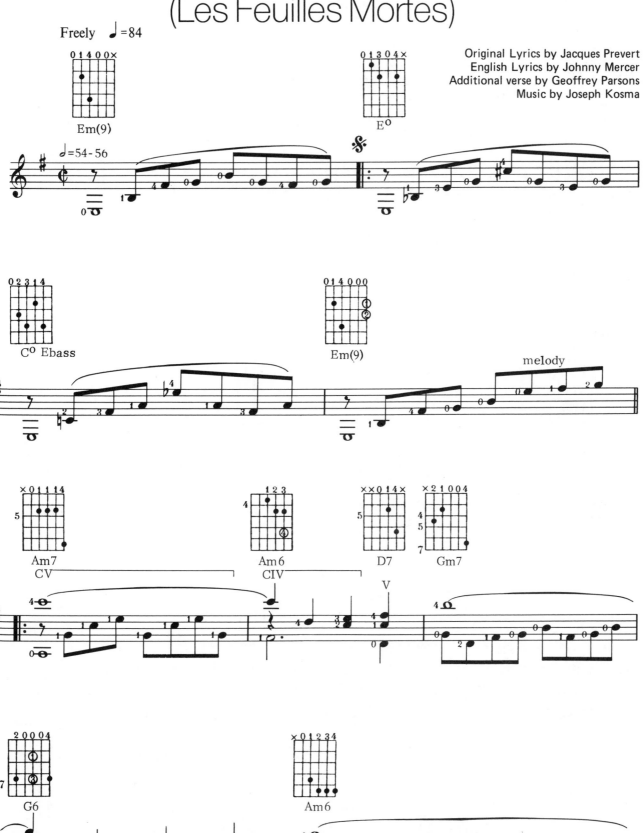

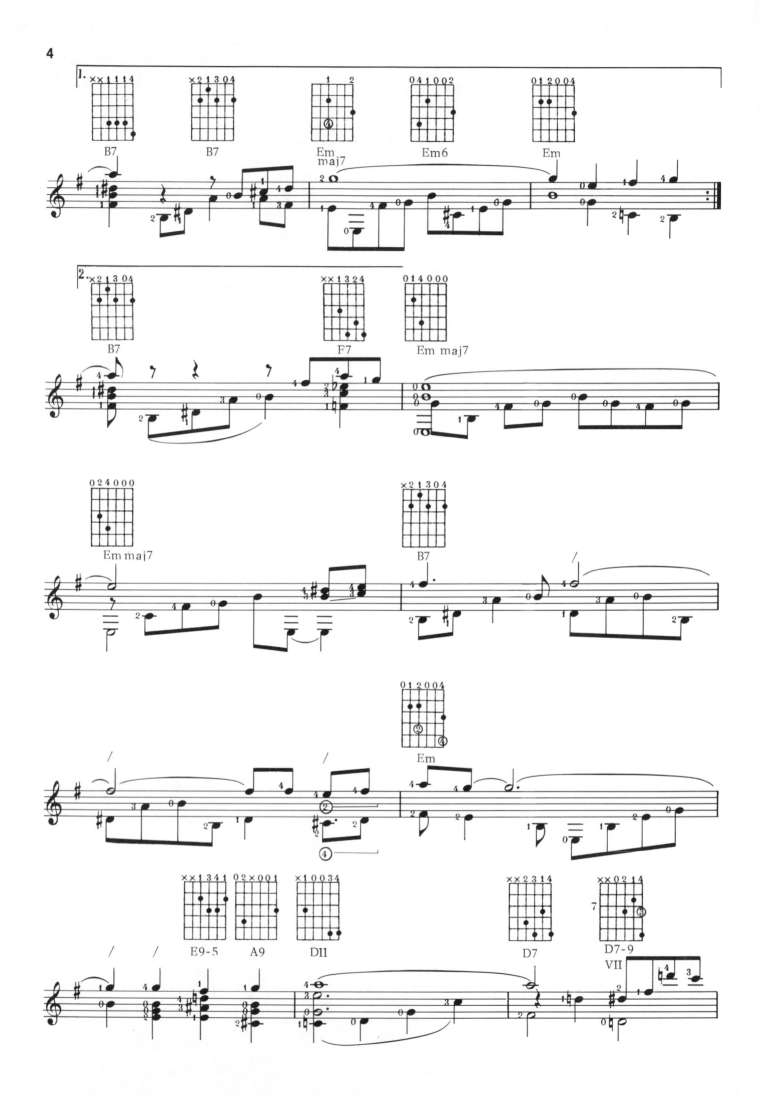

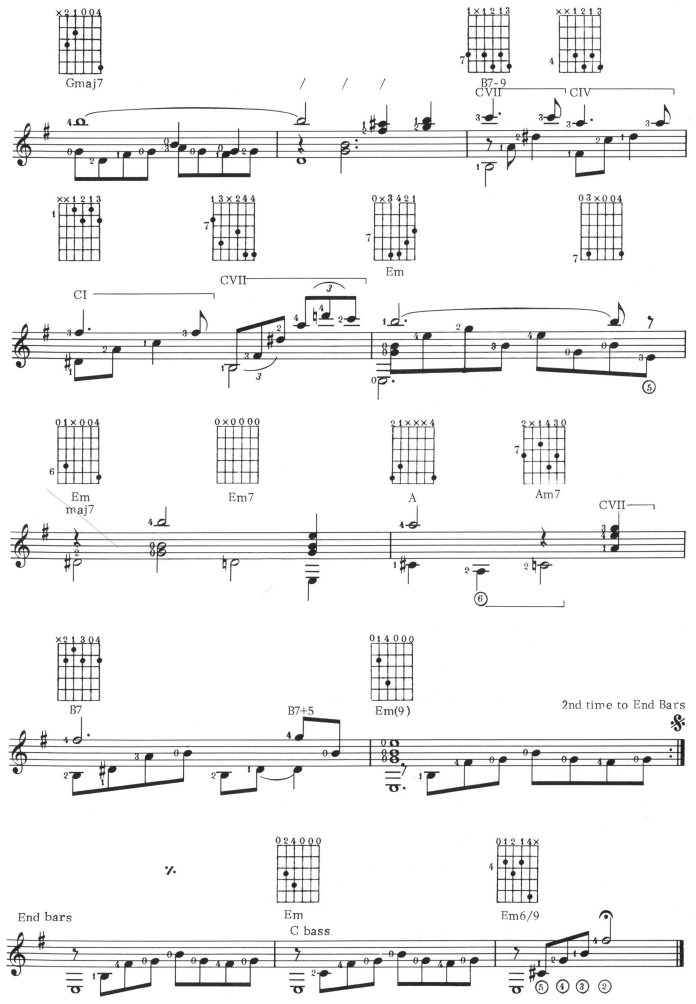

Feelings

Words & Music by Morris Albert

8

I Only Have Eyes For You

Words by Al Dubin
Music by Harry Warren

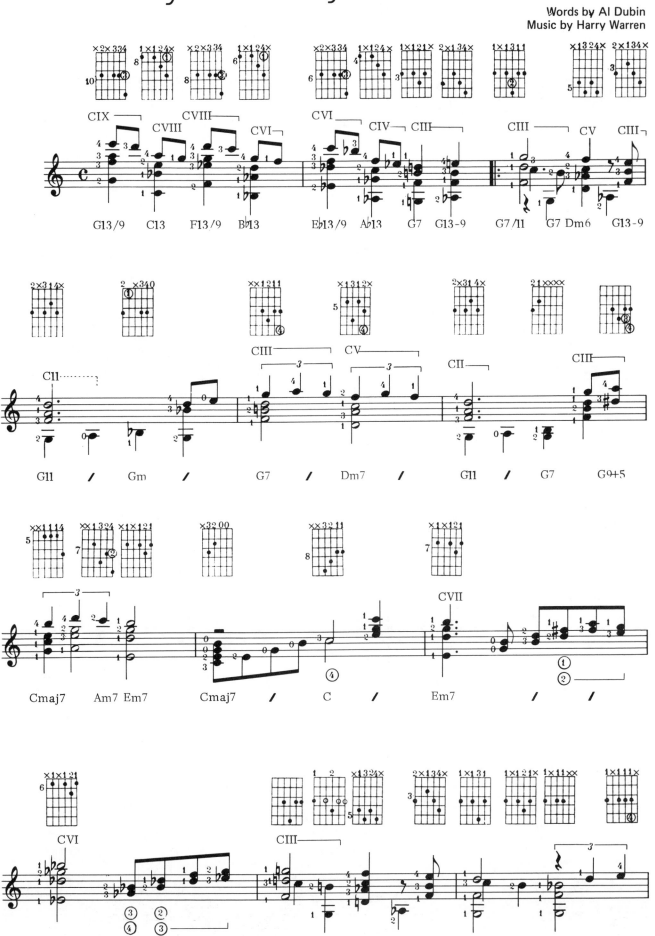

10

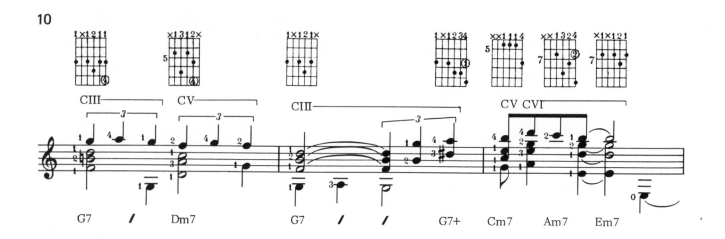

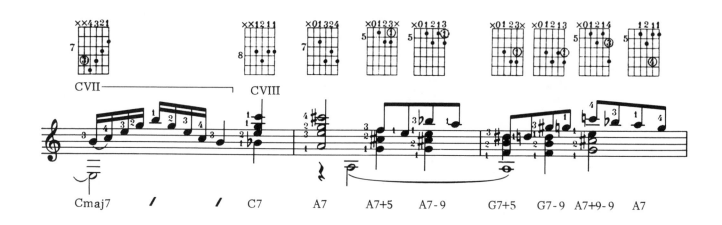

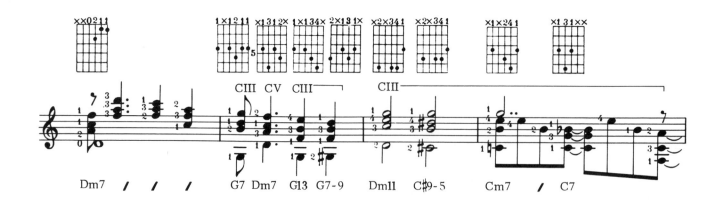

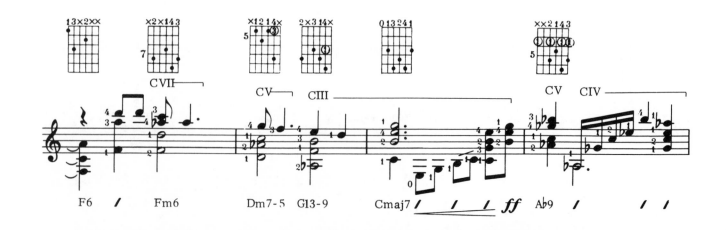

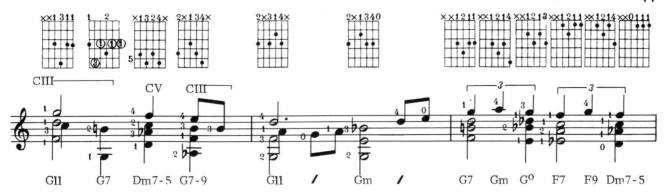

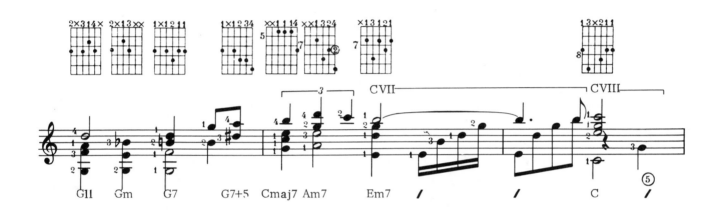

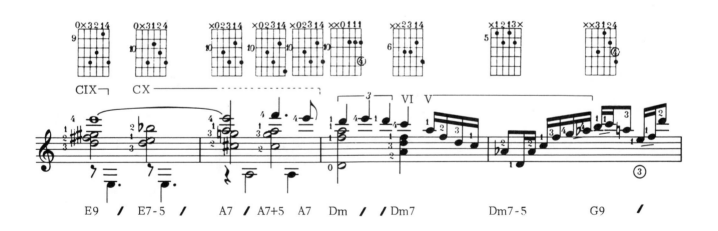

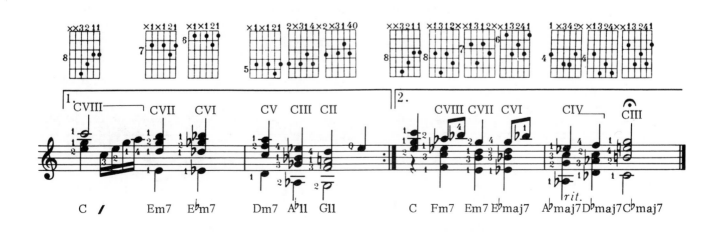

Snowbird

Words & Music by Gene Maclellan

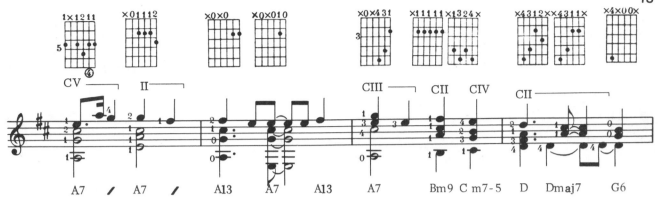

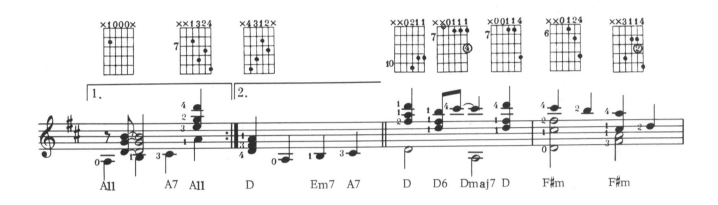

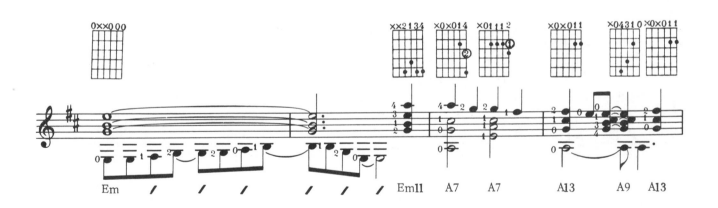

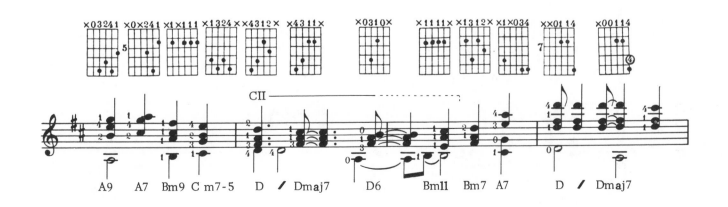

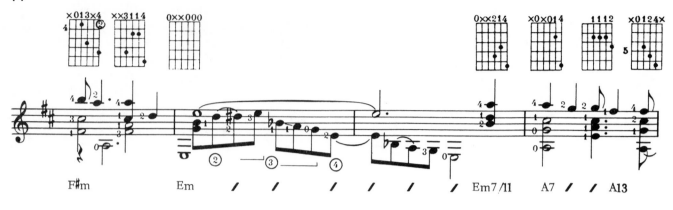

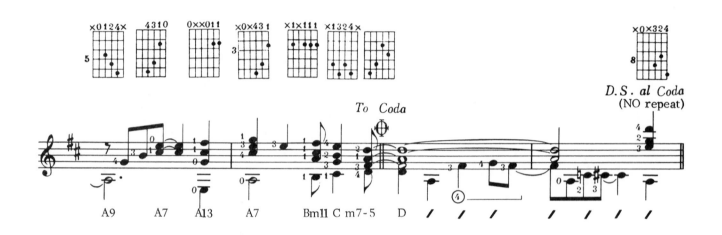

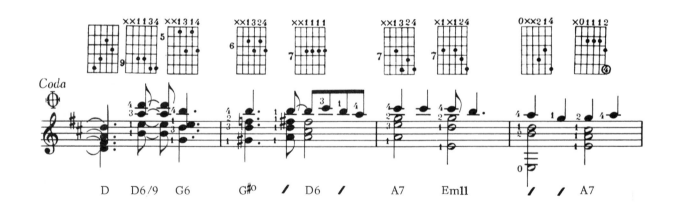

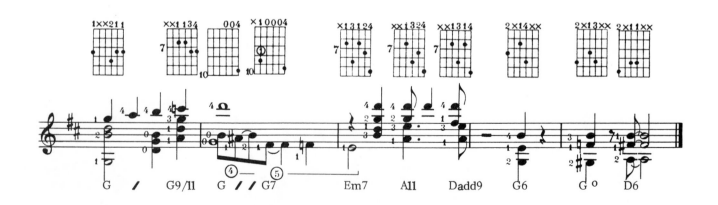

Cavatina

Music by Stanley Myers

Little Green Apples

Words & Music by Bobby Russell

20

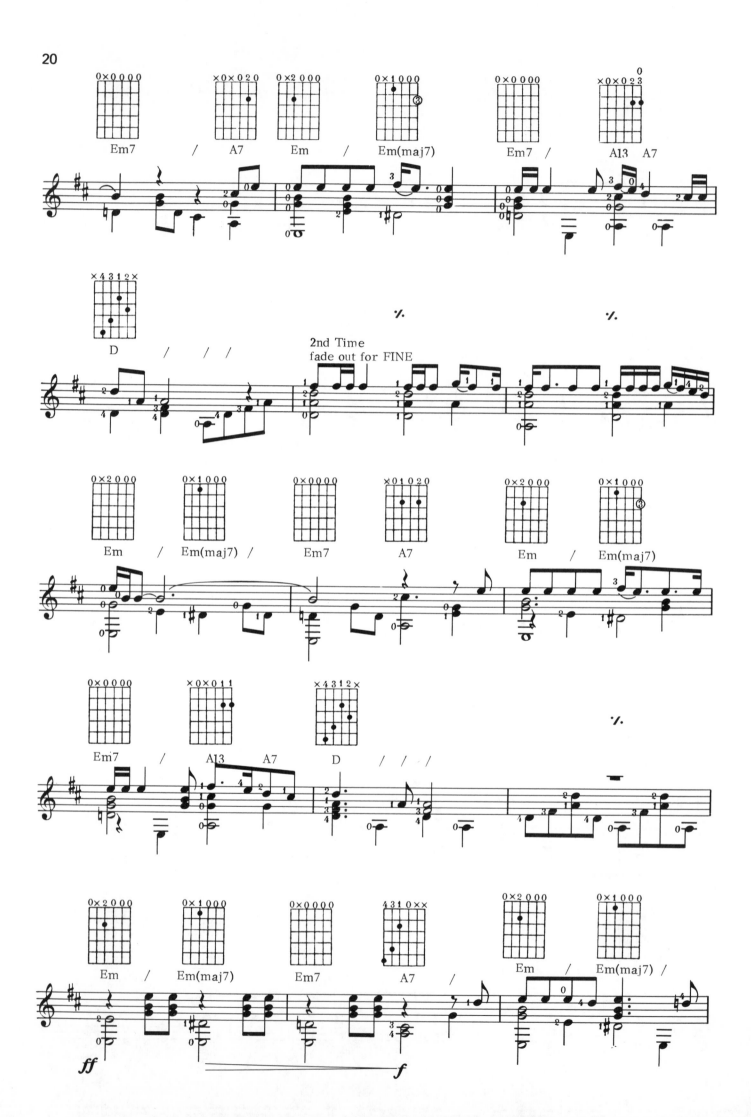

Hello

Words & Music
by Lionel Ritchie

Freely and flowing

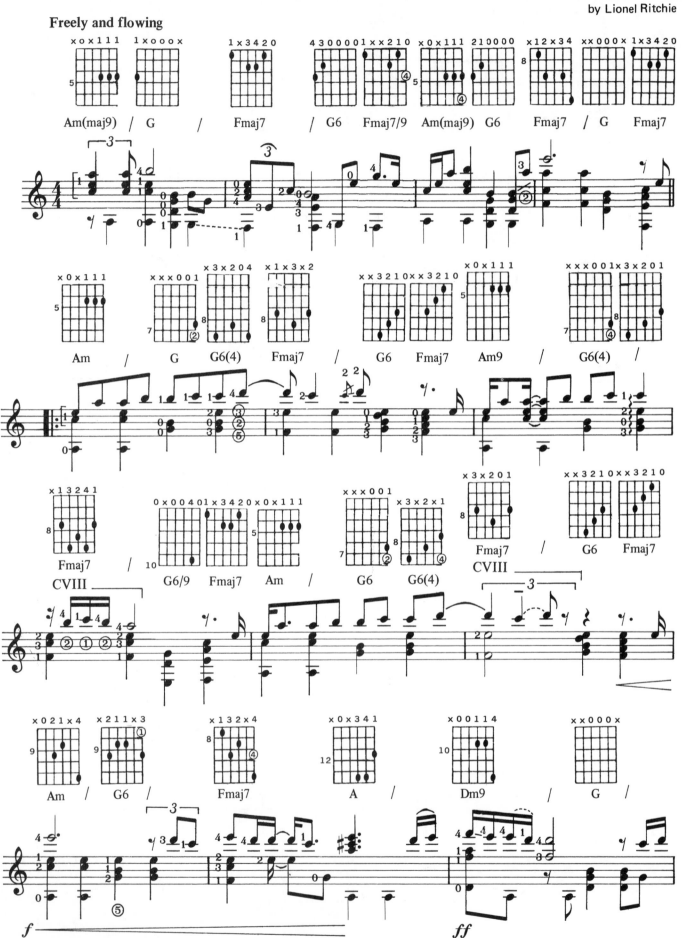

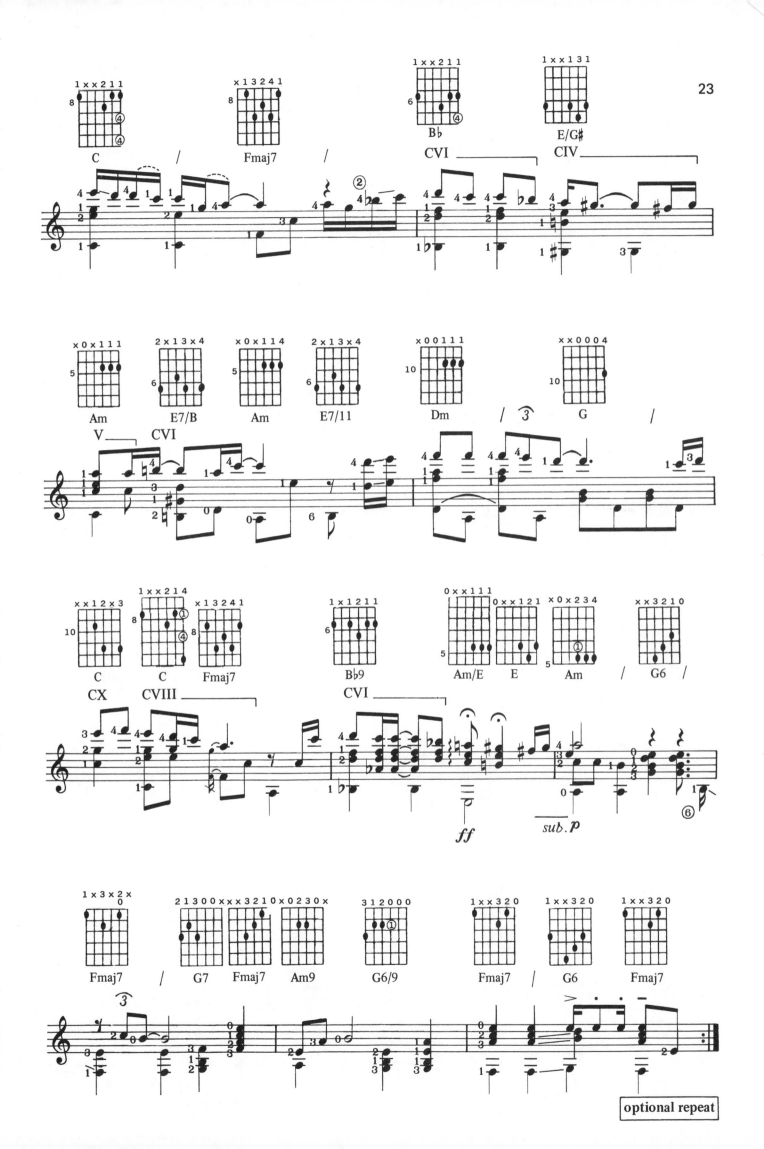

optional repeat

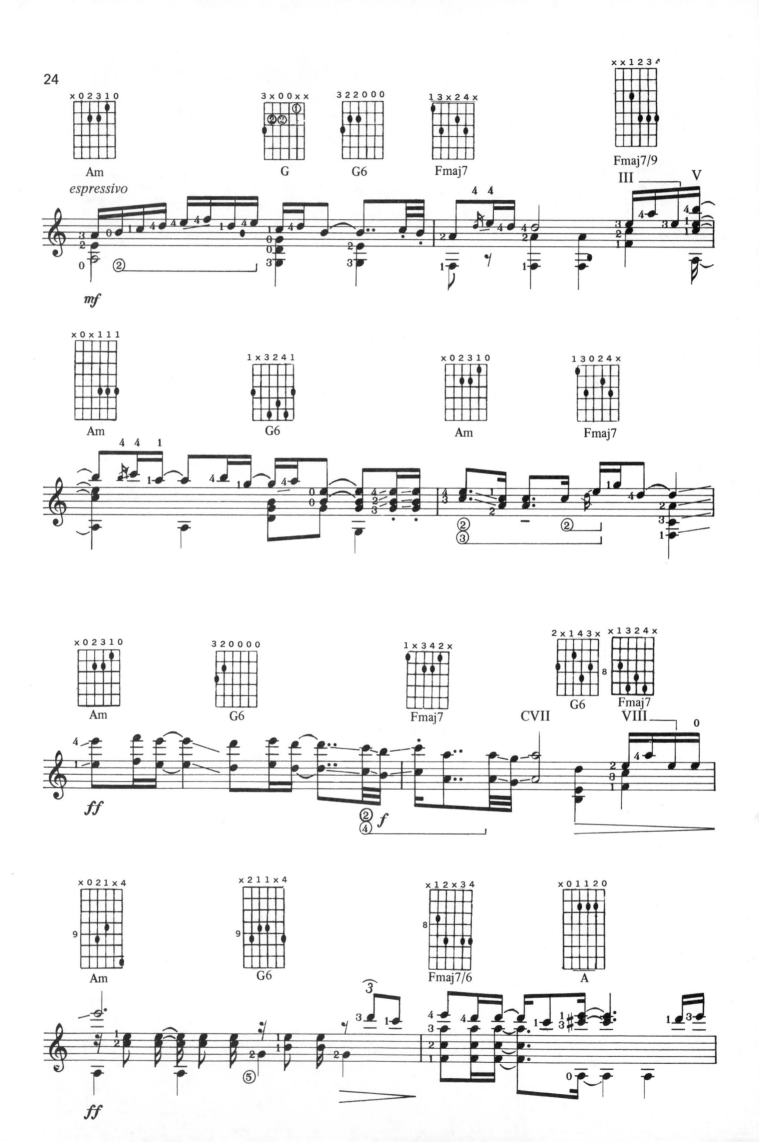

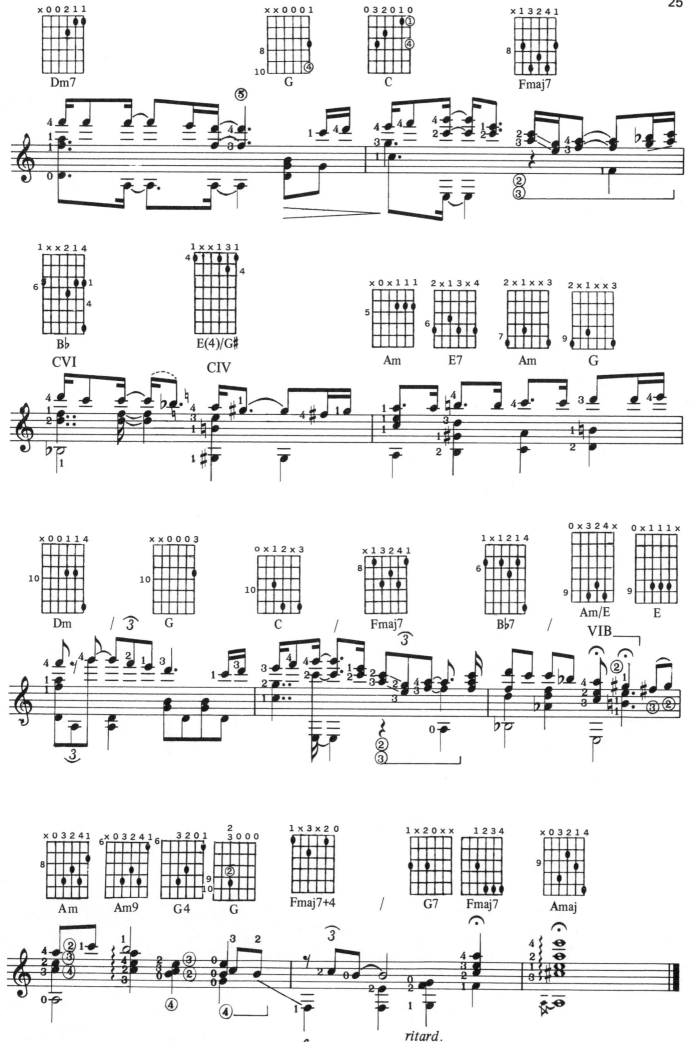

Born Free

Words by Don Black
Music by John Barry

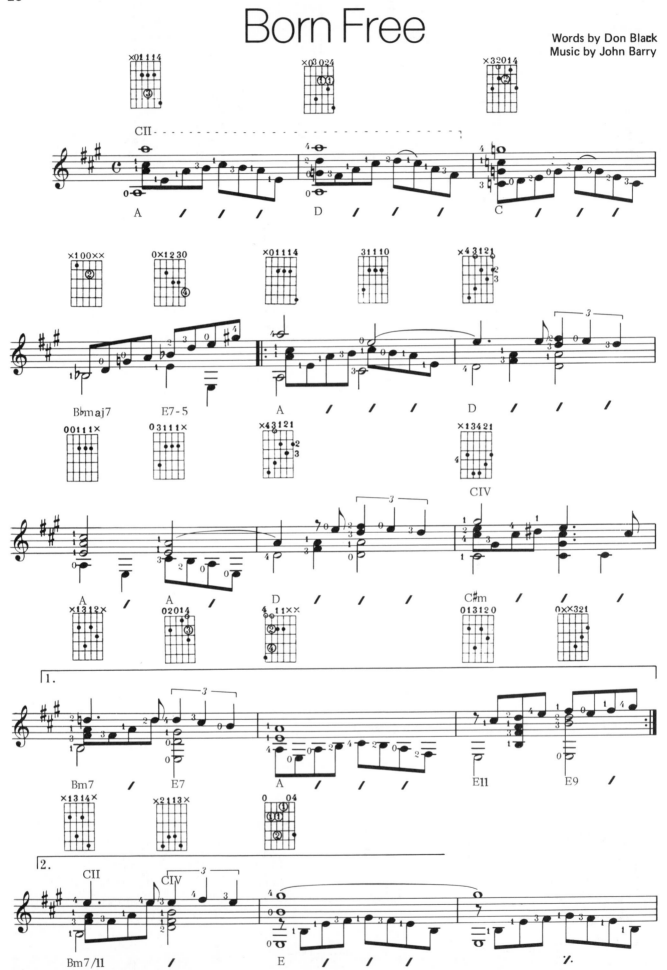

The Way We Were

Words & Music by Marvin Hamlisch/
Marilyn Bergman & J. A. Bergman

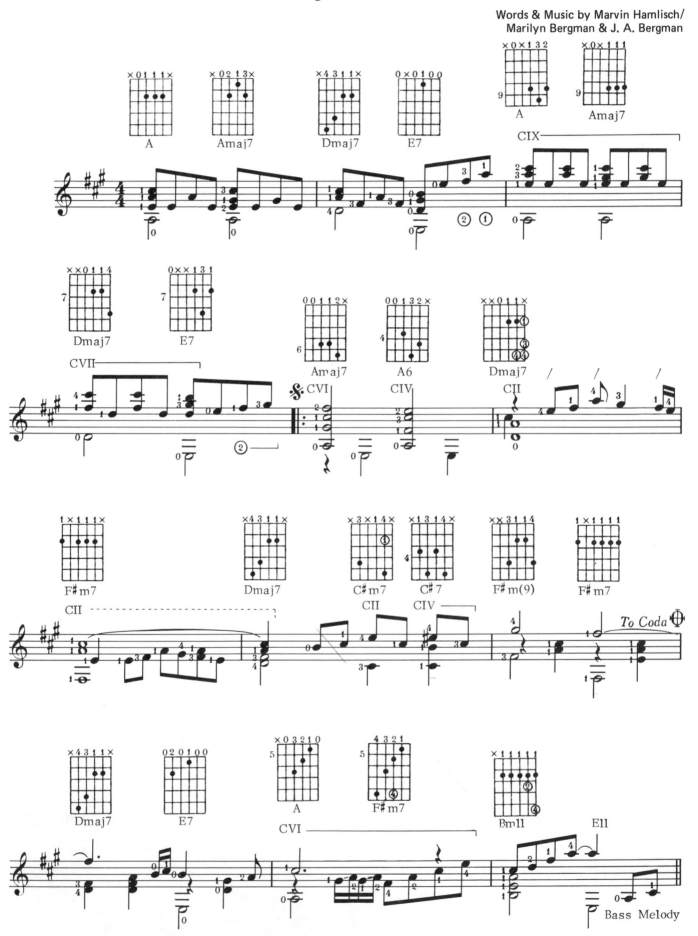

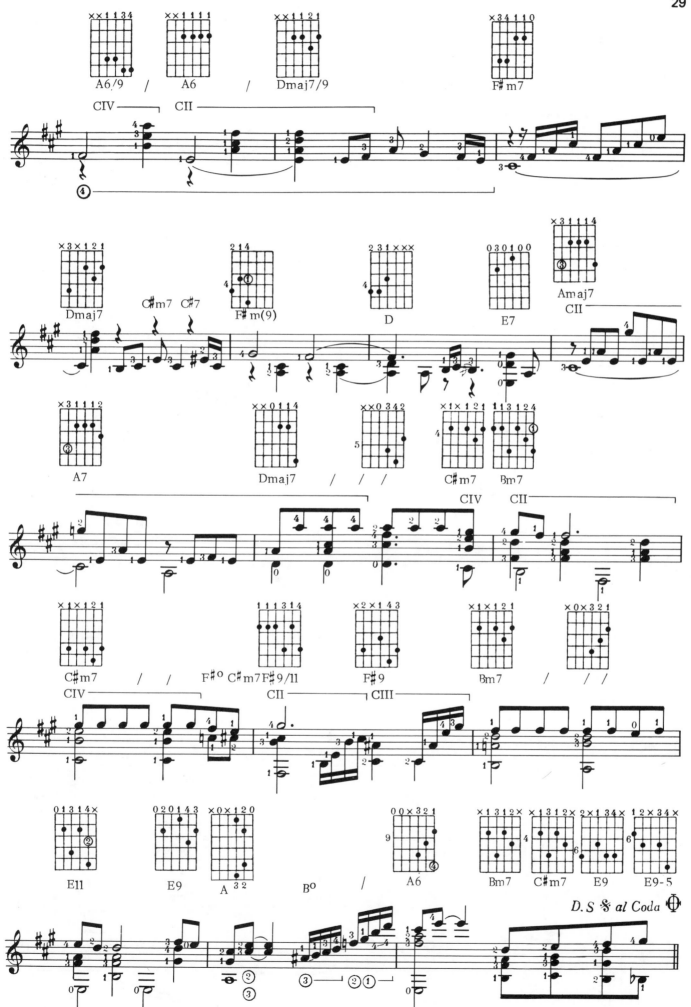

Slow arpeggio

Stand By Your Man

Words & Music
by Tammy Wynette & Billy Sherrill

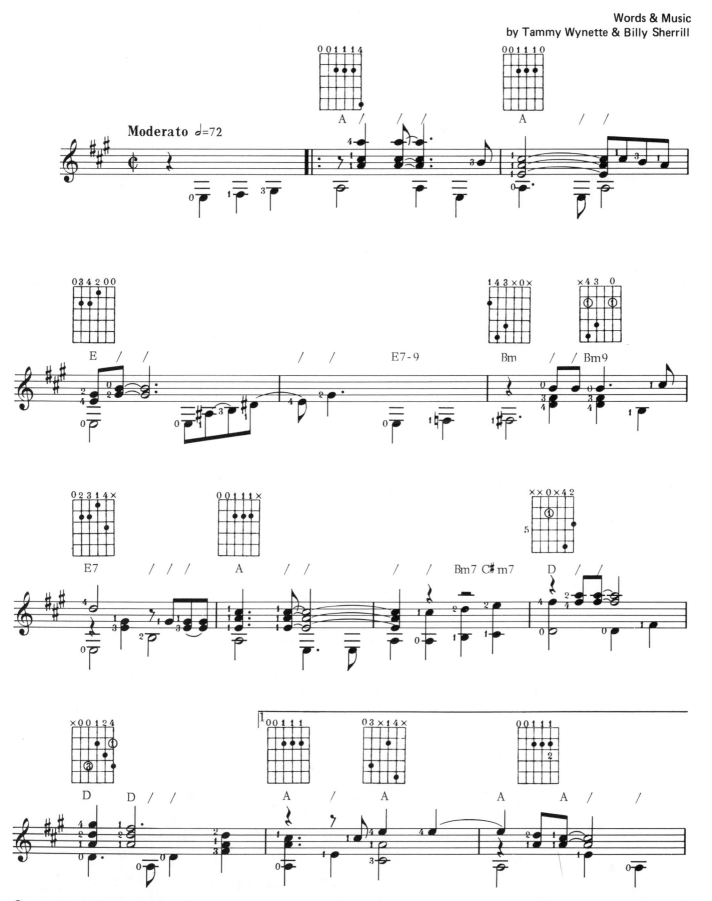

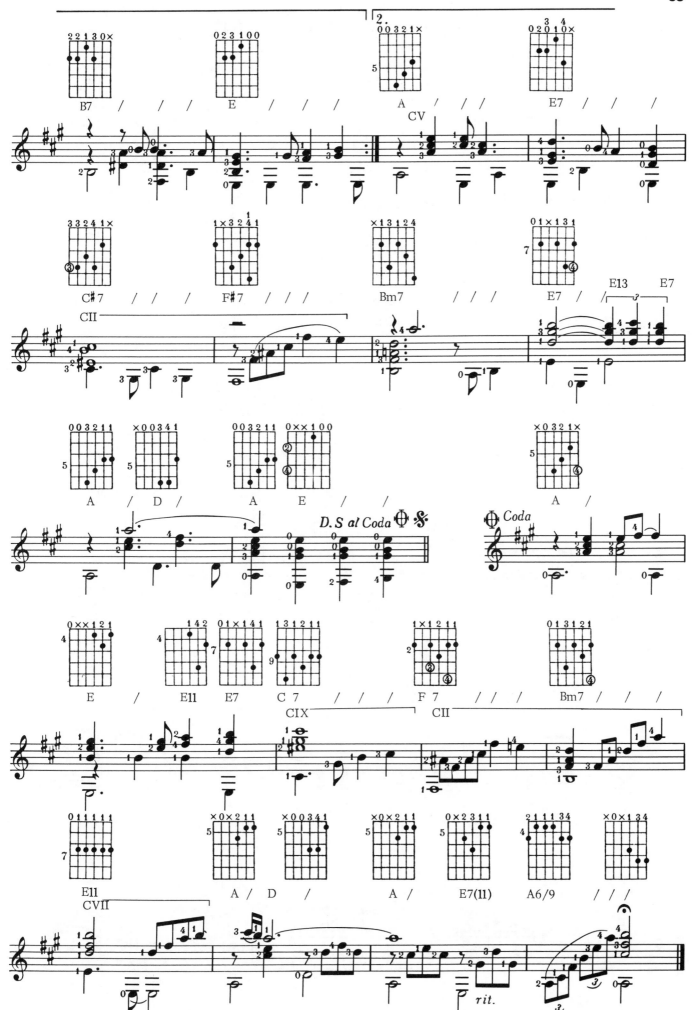

Help Me Make It
Through The Night

Words & Music by Kris Kristofferson

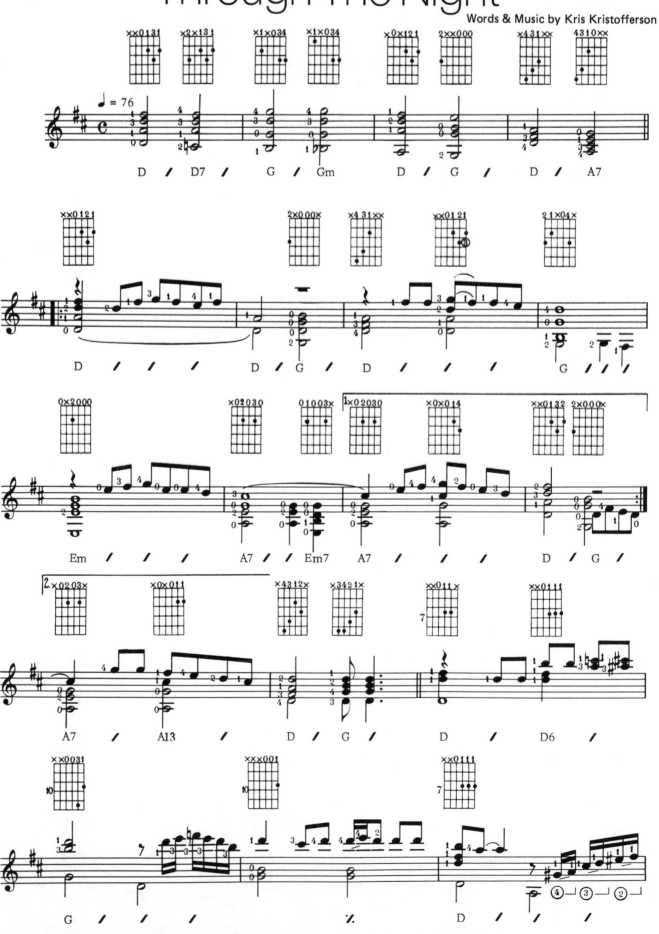

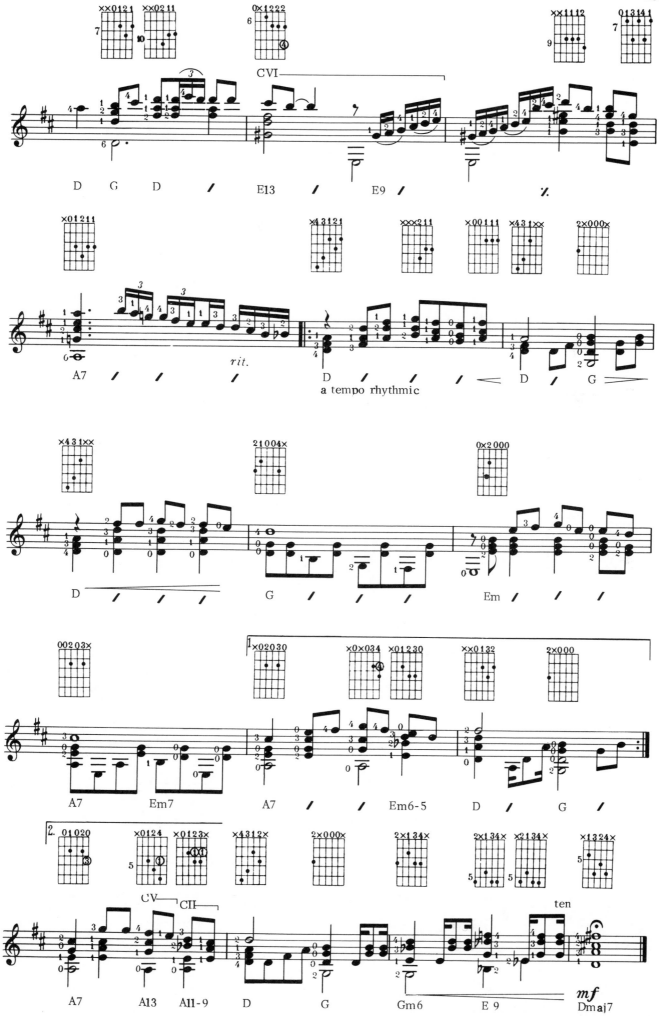

Are You Lonesome Tonight?

Words & Music
by Roy Turk & Lou Handman

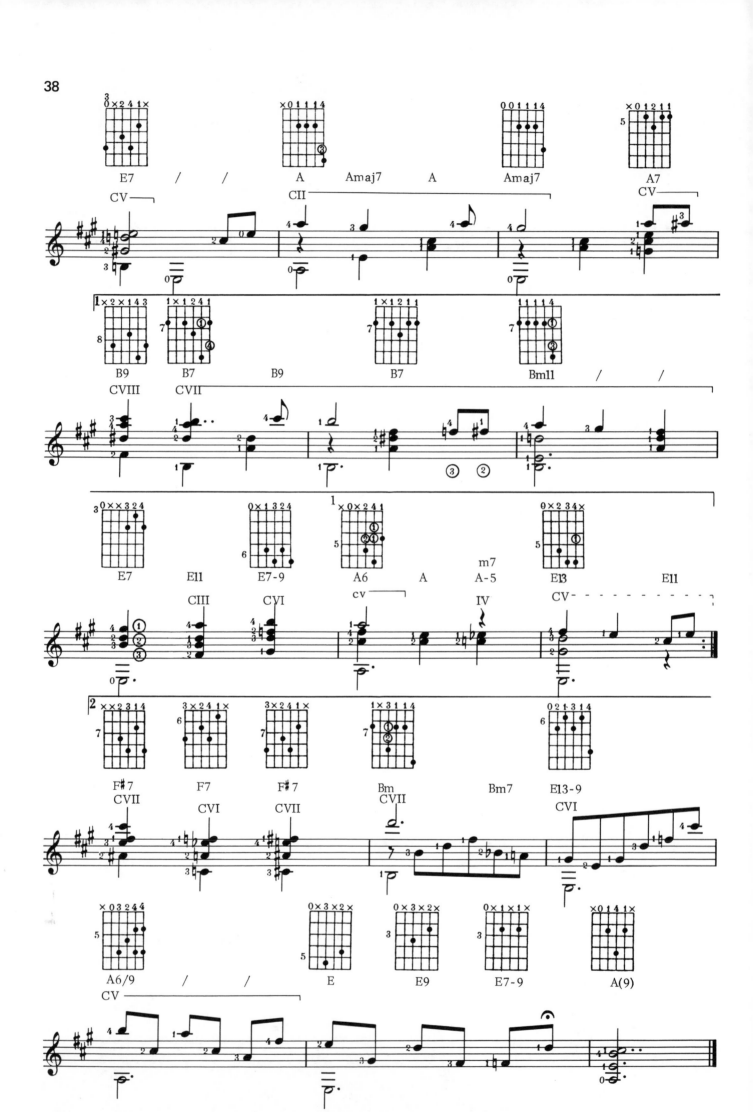

Autumn Concerto

Original Lyrics by Danpa
English Lyrics by John Turner/Geoffrey Parsons & Paul Siegel
Music by C. Bargoni

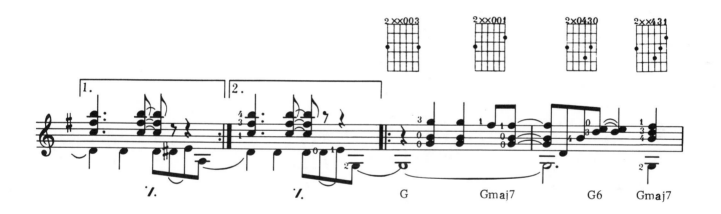

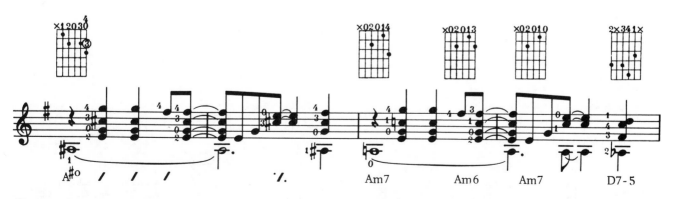

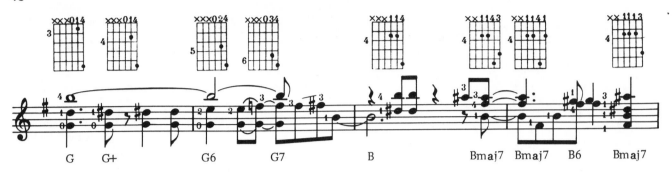

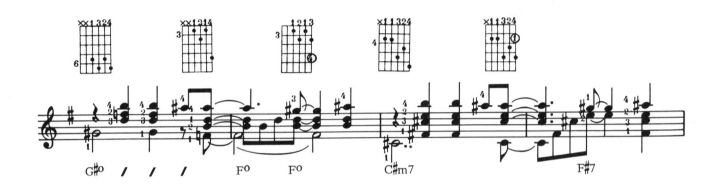

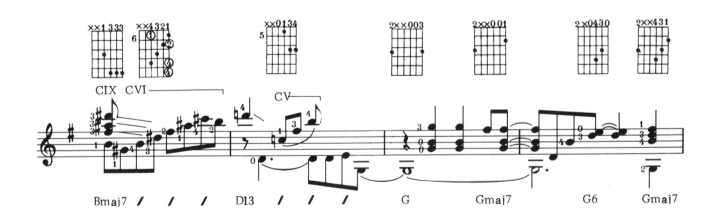

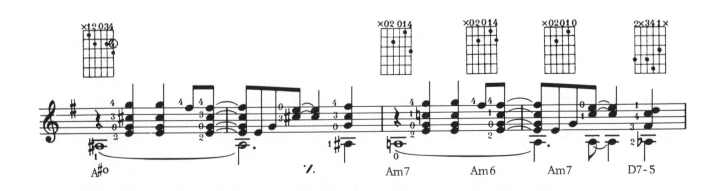

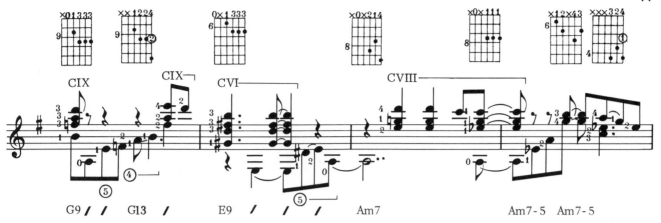

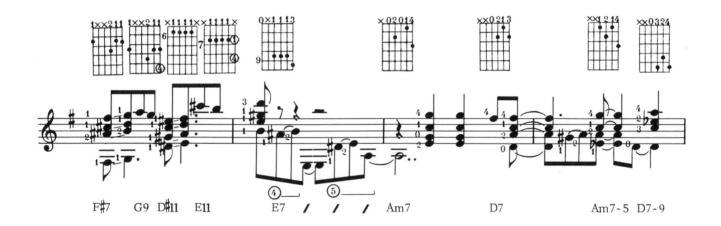

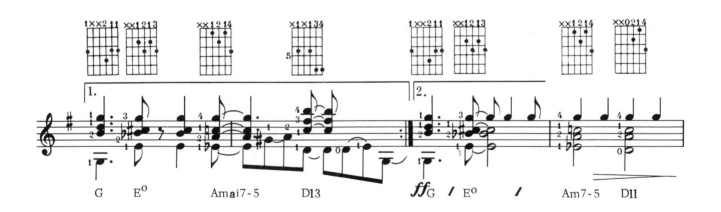

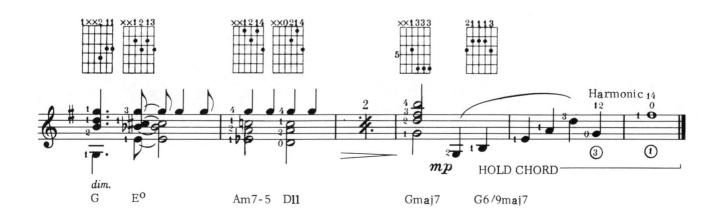

Manhatten

Words by L. Hart
Music by R. Rogers

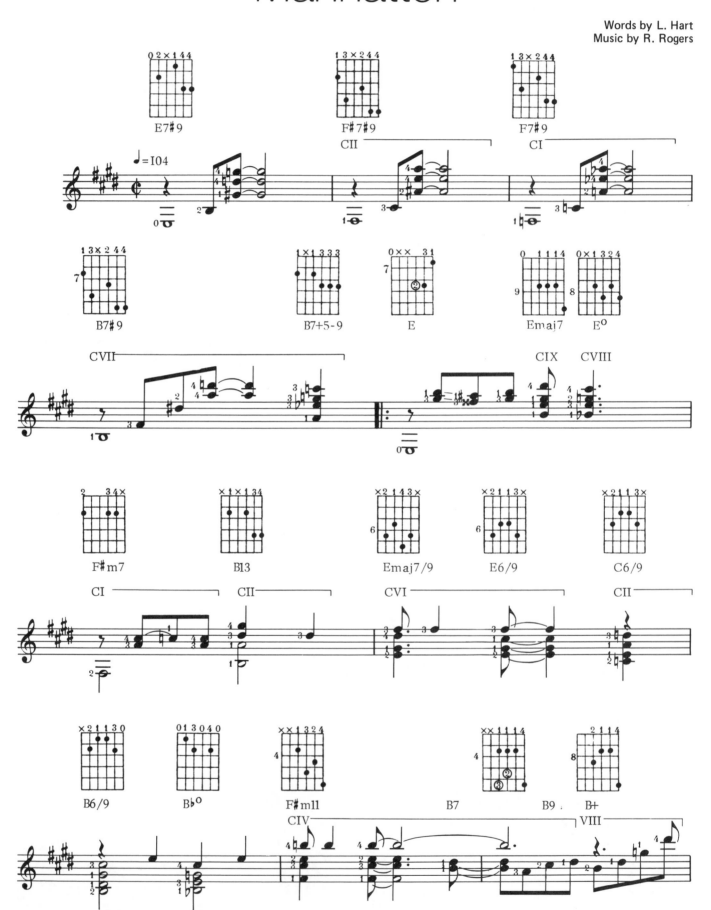

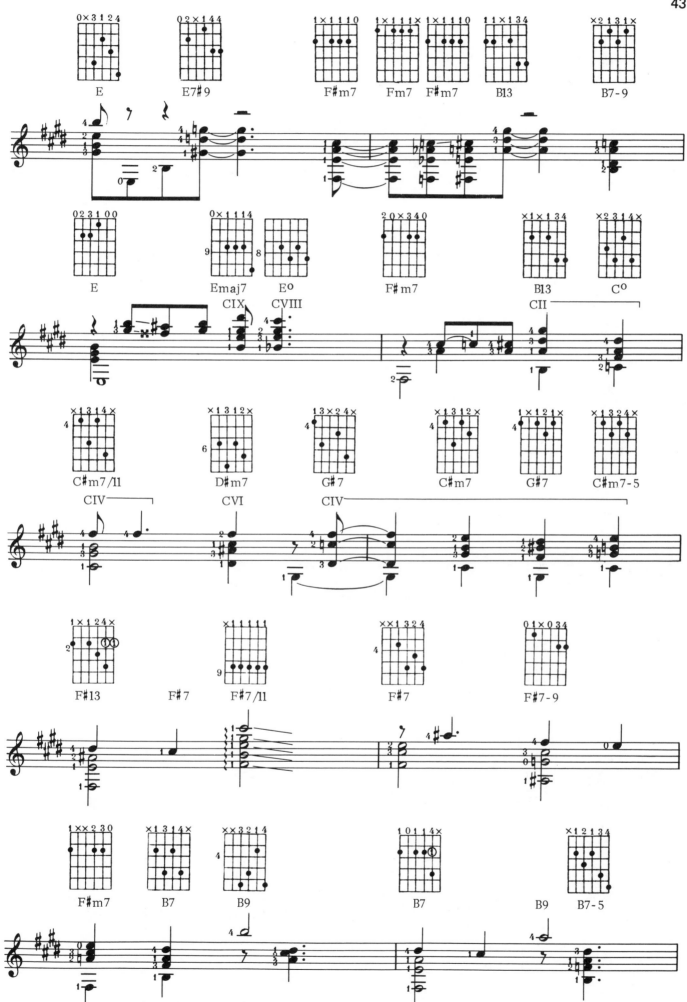

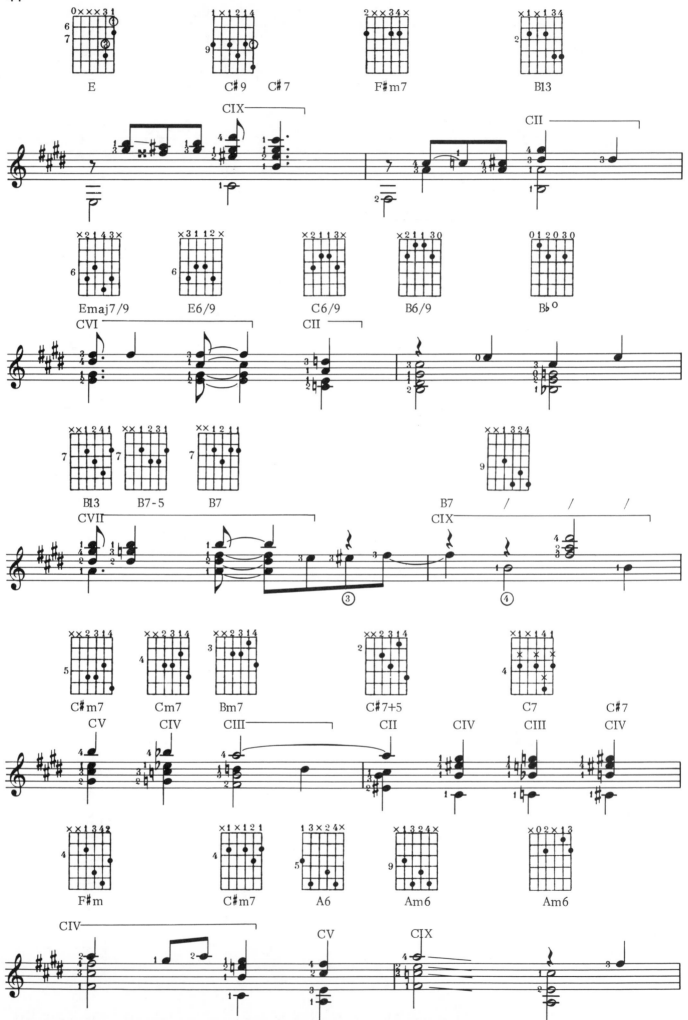

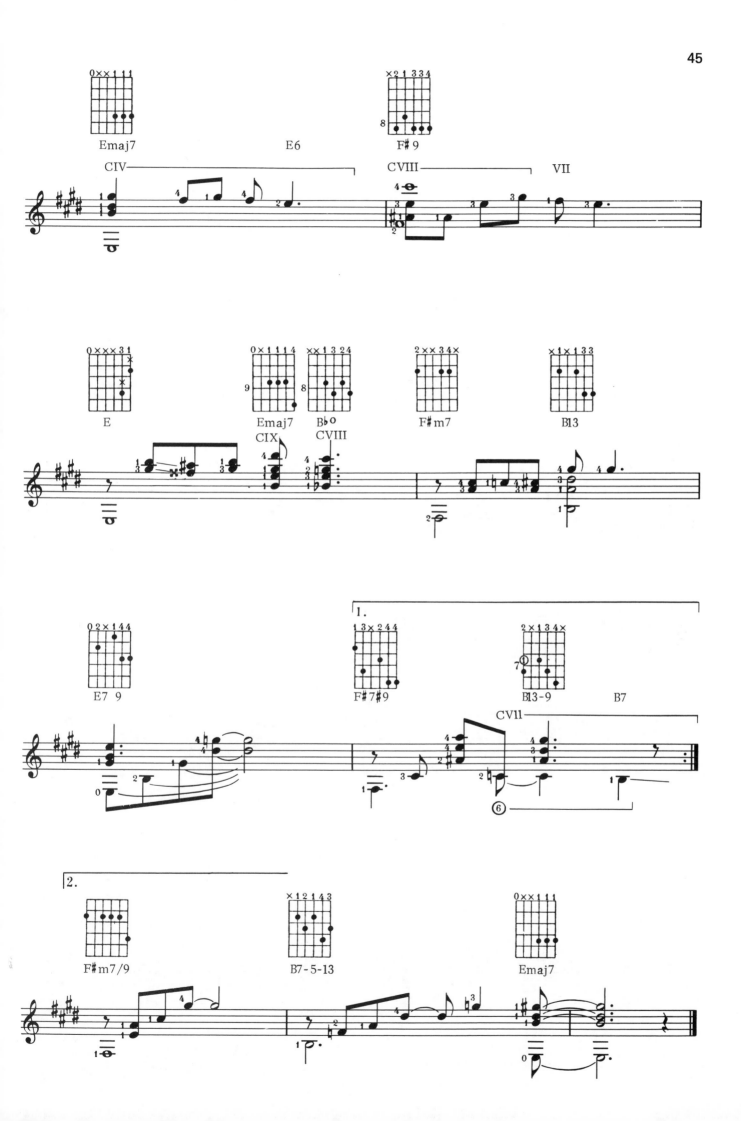

If

Words & Music by David Gates

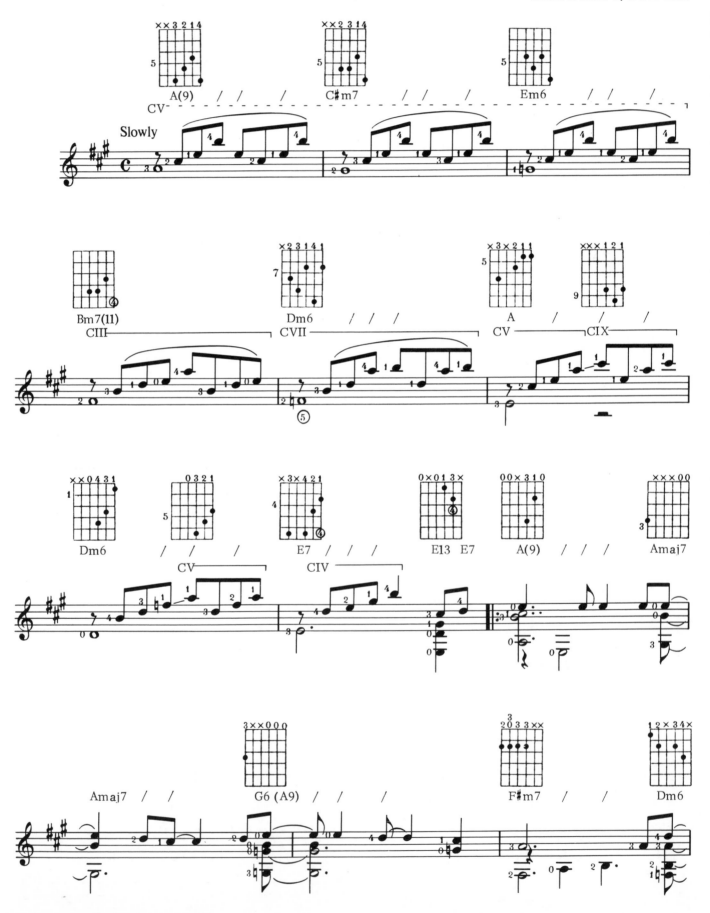

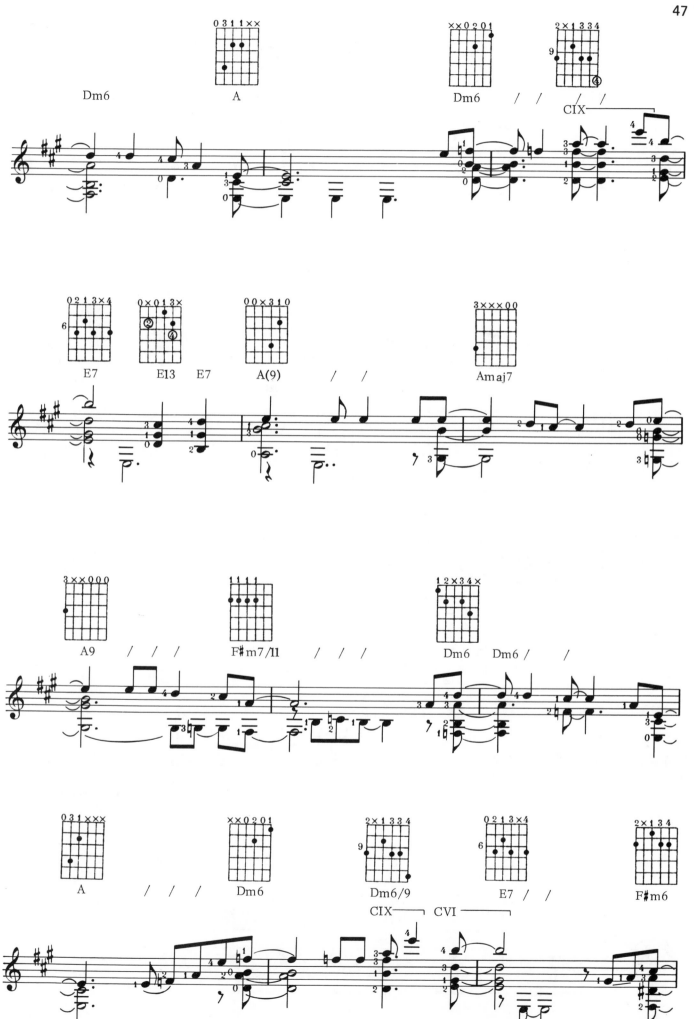

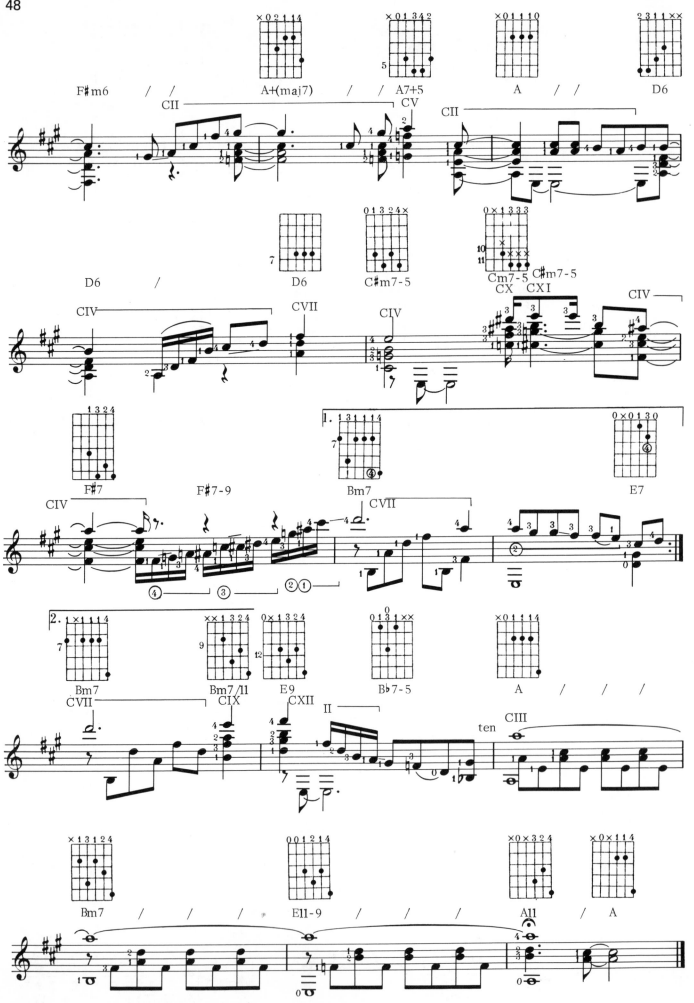